Photography from Sandie Powner Photography & Canva images

Congratulations!

If you're reading this book you've probably got a young puppy.

There's nothing quite like the soft, sweet smelling, fluff and fun of a puppy - you may well be tired from sleepless nights and constantly running around after them, but I promise it will be worth it!

Puppies come with a whole host of challenges and one of the first, and most painful, is puppy biting. I hope you find this book invaluable in helping you to overcome the initial struggles and allow you to move on to the next part of your journey together.

Debbie

debbiepotter.co.uk

About Debbie

As well as living alongside three retrievers, Debbie also shares life with two teenage daughters and her husband - therefore has experience of welcoming both children and puppies into a household, and all the many tribulations this brings!

Debbie is the Founder, Director and Head Trainer at Potter Paws, an independent dog training school specialising in helping people have the ideal dog for their family.

Her passions include puppies, loose-lead training and scent detection. She is passionate about coaching families to be successful in their dog-parenting role and helping create confident, skilled humans and dogs to make every day life a little easier - ensuring you and your best friend have the best life together.

When dog owners are looking for the perfect family dog, the first breeds they think of are normally Labradors or Golden Retrievers, because they're laid-back and easy to fit in to family life. They have a reputation for being great with kids and you often see labs and goldies as the quintessential family dog as portrayed in film and tv.

But the reality can be quite different.

"Dogs do speak but only to those who know how to listen"

~

Orhan Pamuk

Like any dog, it takes dedication and consistency to train even the most laid back Labrador and create a happy, well-adjusted family pet. Even the best of breeds can end up being in a nightmare situation if not understood and managed correctly.

That's where Debbie can help! She specialises in helping families create a consistent, positive environment for their dog to grow and flourish, working with the characteristics of retrieving breeds to help them become the much-loved member of the family, that you've always dreamed of.

There's so much more to owning a dog than simply teaching him to sit - which is often a revelation - as Debbie helps owners to realise that the human end of the lead is more important than you might initially think. Living with a dog can be emotional and overwhelming, so supporting the humans with their own outlook is crucial to training success.

debbiepotter.co.uk

OUCH!

Your guide to surviving puppy biting

by Debbie Potter

Contents

Introduction

I was 4 years old when we welcomed our first dog, Tess, to the family and we rescued a further two, Tyler and Charlie, whilst I was still at home, all were older at around 1 - 2 years. When I moved into my own home and had my first 'own' dog, Leo, he was another rescue and 2 years old, so I had no experience of puppy biting or puppies in general.

At the very beginning of my journey to become a dog trainer, when my children were 6 & 8 and Leo was a grand age of 13, we welcomed our first puppy, Dave the Labrador, to the family!

I'd always wanted a puppy - it's every girl's dream and even at 32 I was incredibly excited to have my very own puppy. Naturally I wanted to show him off to everyone and spoil him rotten. Despite having some initial knowledge and doing lots of reading prior to his arrival, I wasn't prepared for the puppy biting!

Dave was quite a nibbly puppy and it was certainly overwhelming at times. The majority of my jumpers had holes in the sleeves from those sharp puppy teeth and I remember how painful the odd toe nip was – ouch!

The children adored him but naturally were reluctant to interact during the more bitey times of the day, and although he was adorable, the puppy biting didn't quite match the idealistic image I expected of life with a puppy.

Thankfully, Dave grew out of it quite quickly and by the time he was around 6 months old the puppy biting was a thing of the past - phew!

By the time I was ready to welcome my next puppy to the gang, I had racked up a lot more experience, knowledge and understanding of puppies and their needs. In comparison, Rem was a dream, I don't remember him ever nipping, although he had a whole host of other issues that again taught me a new skill set and literally changed our lives (for the better) - but that's a topic for another book!

Due to my experiences and ever growing knowledge, I had much more understanding of the warning signs and when to start the calming process (before the biting ever happens). The latest addition, Fred barely nipped at all and was possibly the most relaxed puppy out of the three, although he definitely made up for it as a teenager!

Now of course these differences can be down to the individual puppy's character and genetics, but how you and your family approach issues like puppy biting can also have a large impact on your puppy's journey and learning experiences.

I appreciate that as a new puppy parent, you may not have had numerous previous puppies to help you learn what to do and what not to do, equally you will not have the time or inclination to devote to learning everything about puppies. That's why this book has been created.

The learning and techniques I have used with my own puppies are explored within this book. I hope they help you on the road to success with your own cuddly puppy and make your journey through puppy hood a little less painful.

What we will learn

In this guide to surviving puppy biting we will explore many areas, including:

- Why puppies mouth and nip
- How to satisfy their need to mouth
- How to manage their world and set them up to succeed
- How to be prepared
- What to do to reduce or manage your puppy mouthing
- What to do when they are being nippy and biting
- Discover games and activities that you can enjoy with your puppy to help reduce biting

You will need...
TIME, PATIENCE & CONSISTENCY!

Firstly, there is no magic wand or quick fix when it comes to training your puppy. You will need to allow time for your puppy to develop and learn, and have patience to stick with a method not just for a day but for weeks/months. You will need to remain consistent in your approach every day and also ensure your family members are consistent with you.

The tips provided in this book are designed to help you manage and reduce mouthing in young puppies in a family home. Every puppy is different and they will stop and start nipping at different ages, but we are generally speaking about puppies that are around 4 - 6 months old. Most puppies will have grown out of the mouthing and nipping by 7 months.

The following pages will give you the knowledge and practical advice to help reduce puppy biting effectively. We aim to provide you with information to enable you to take a proactive approach, which is more beneficial than waiting until your puppy is biting and then only reacting to the problem.

One important thing to note is that although many people refer to it as 'biting', in most cases puppies are simply mouthing and nipping as would be a natural communication in their litter. The term biting can seem quite 'extreme' and lead us to think of aggression rather than development.

Puppy nipping is normal! It is a normal part of your puppy journey and part of owning a puppy. Yes, it is hard work and it's not enjoyable to have a 'shark' puppy. So, let's look at how we overcome this stage as quickly as possible.

Mouthing is important, it needs to happen. We will rarely be able to fully stop our puppy from doing it but we can learn how to manage it to make it better. It's our job as canine companions to support and guide our puppy through this stage and help them transition on to the rest of their training journey.

The facts

Just like people, dogs have two sets of teeth in their lifetime. The first 'puppy' set, which comprises 28 sharp needle-like teeth, grow between 2 - 6 weeks old.

They start to lose their puppy teeth between 12-16 weeks old and will lose all of these puppy teeth and have grown their full set of adult teeth by around 6 months old.

Adult dogs have 42 teeth.

Just like babies and children the teething process is painful and can cause a lack of appetite and irritability.

You will rarely find puppy teeth as they are super tiny and often fall out whilst they are eating or playing.

Due to the different bacteria in dogs mouths they rarely get cavities, however gum disease is much more common.

When dogs have their adult set of teeth, it is important to ensure the teeth and gums are looked after to prevent any issues in the future.

This may include regular teeth cleaning using a brush and toothpaste, giving chews to naturally clean or adding supplements in their diet to reduce plaque.

Why it happens

It's easy to think that you have a broken, aggressive, or not normal puppy when all you see on instagram is cute bundles of fluff and people appearing quite happy - surely their puppy never bites! I assure you they probably do but people rarely share that side of life with a puppy. First we'll explore WHY puppies use their teeth!

- It is normal puppy behaviour
- To communicate, interact and initiate interaction
- To navigate their world and the people/things in it
- To explore and learn
- For pain relief when teething
- It can be rewarding for them

Understanding the reason behind WHY your puppy mouths will help you to see that it isn't being naughty or deliberately causing harm. This alone can transform your approach to puppy biting.

During the teething process, which takes place approximately between 3 - 6 months old, your puppy will be feeling very sore and experiencing discomfort due to the movement of the teeth in their gums. Just like with babies, your puppy will become irritable, they can't express this so we see changes in their behaviour as a result. When your puppy starts biting and chewing, they are often trying to sooth their gums to feel better.

Communicating by mouthing is normal for all puppies - it's how puppies communicate with their litter mates and mum in the initial stages. If your puppy has only just arrived at your home and has spent two months with a litter of puppies learning how to communicate and interact with other dogs, they only know how to mouth/bite to 'speak'. Puppies interact by mouthing, nipping and biting to try and initiate an action or reaction and play fight with the other puppies, and that's all they know. They've been taken from that world and suddenly have to learn that humans don't respond in the same way as their litter mates would have. Humans don't like it when puppy nips and nibbles and it's our responsibility to help our puppy learn the differences between one species (their litter mates) and another (their humans).

It's common to have an 'easy' first week and then to suddenly feel overwhelmed with a more challenging puppy. It takes puppies a few days to settle in and feel comfortable so some normal behaviours will be suppressed whilst they get to grips with their new environment.

Puppy interactions can seem quite rough. Play between dogs can seem quite mouthy and bitey, but it is very rare for puppies to be aggressive. It can happen on occasion, but it is not normal for puppies to show aggression towards humans, so if you're concerned about anything, please seek professional individual support for your puppy.

TOP TIP: In the useful information section at the end of this book you'll find a list of websites/organisations to help you start looking for a reputable trainer

Aside from communication, when calm mouthing turns into a bite it is often puppies attempting to interact or reduce frustration. Sucking, mouthing, nipping, chewing all provide stress relief and release tension (which is held in the jaw) and therefore attempting to nip hands/people is often a sign that puppies are attempting to obtain relief from their emotions.

In the long term, if your puppy does something more than once, it's likely to be because it was rewarding the first time – it got them a desired result, was something that felt good or had an enjoyable consequence.

What we need to do is consider WHY they find it rewarding and discover other ways they can get that same reward and provide it for them. Puppies think it's perfectly acceptable to nibble and mouth people, and it is what people expect when they have a puppy, BUT as an adult dog it is NOT acceptable. This means we need to show them and teach them to find alternative ways to satisfy their needs and make themselves feel good and rewarded, because it won't be tolerated when they are an adult dog. The sooner we do this, the easier our journey.

How to satisfy their need

We know puppies are going to mouth. It is impossible and detrimental to stop them doing it completely because we want them to have opportunities to interact and explore the world, BUT we can show them what they should mouth and chew on and encourage them to chew on the RIGHT things, so they learn that chewing/biting on the suitable item is more rewarding than nibbling people.

What can my puppy chew on?

- Puppy chew toys (soft and harder items)
- Frozen damp tea towels (to aid teething)
- Stuffed KONGS (hide food inside)
- Edible natural chews (pizzles, tendons, dried ears, raw bones – AVOID rawhide!)

We can provide suitable outlets for chewing. One of my favourite ways is to provide plenty of edible natural chews with no additives or preservatives. They taste good so puppies want to chew them and get an instant reward and satisfaction from doing so. Make sure you supervise so they learn how to take their time and not chew them up too quickly.

When looking at different chew items, ask yourself:

Will my puppy WANT to chew on this?

If you only provide plastic bone shaped items they are unlikely to choose to chew on these as there is little reward. Dried, edible and natural chews are the most beneficial. If you're not sure whether an item is natural, the ingredients on the label should give you an indication of this.

Avoid giving your puppy or adult dog rawhide as this is a biproduct of the leather industry. It is readily available in many pet shops but is often treated with colour and chemicals to look more attractive but can actually be quite dangerous for dogs to eat.

By providing your puppy with a suitable chew you are showing them what to do – don't mouth/nip/bite on that, chew on this instead. They are getting the reward and satisfaction of chewing but on the right things rather than on our slippers, table legs or furniture. Therefore we are creating a new satisfying behaviour and in future they will choose to do the appropriate behaviour/activity to get the desired result.

What is a suitable edible chew?

Edible chews are ones that are designed to be fully ingested and eaten. In general they are made from dried animal body parts or products which are not only healthy but also tasty, which results in your dog wanting to chew them rather than your hand.

We can generally place the different chew items into three categories, Easy, Medium & Hard.

EASY

Something that is relatively soft to chew
Takes minimal effort and provides an instant satisfaction
May only last your puppy a minute or two
Provides a quick, easy 'hit' of satisfaction

Examples: rabbit ear, jerky, tripe sticks, 'spaghetti', fish skin

MEDIUM

Slightly harder to chew on but still 'easy'
Still provides a fairly instant level of satisfaction
May require a little more effort or be slightly longer lasting
Will give a longer opportunity for stress relief

Examples: pig ear, cow ear, dried skins, pizzle

HARD

Will take a lot more effort to get taste/satisfaction
Much firmer, larger in size
Will last a fairly long time
Unlikely to finish in one sitting so can return to it at a later
point

Examples: Yaker, ostrich bone, buffalo horn, anthos root,
large pizzle

Choosing the right chew for the situation

The first step is to discover which chews your puppy actually likes and doesn't like - every dog is different and will have their own preference. If they are in a super bitey mood, offering a chew that doesn't interest them won't have the desired effect. Do a quick test when they are calm and relaxed by offering the various chew options and seeing which ones they pick first or have a preference for.

If you offer a variety of chews over time you can create a hierarchy of chew items rated from their least to most favourite.

Your aim is to match the chew level to your dog's arousal level so that we are giving them a fair chance of accepting the chew offered. If your dog is calm/relaxed they'll be easily able to accept a medium or hard chew, but if they are over excited/aroused they simply won't be able to think rationally to accept anything other than a very soft chew – they might even need a simple scatter feed first and then a soft chew afterwards.

Chewing is a relaxing behaviour, but your puppy needs to be in a frame of mind to be able to undertake the chewing activity. If they are over-excited they simply will be unable to chew. Chewing will work most effectively as a preventative method. If they are already overstimulated and biting, use a scatter feed to reduce their arousal in the first instance and help them to calm down enough to be able to accept a super easy chew.

Scatter Feed

This is where you take a handful of small yet super tasty treats or kibble and sprinkle them either on the carpet, grass or in a snuffle mat. Your puppy can then use their nose to sniff out the treats. Sniffing is calming and relaxing so can help to lower arousal

Which activity or chew do I offer?

Over-excited puppy

Scatter feed

Food puzzle

Offer an easy chew

Ask for a simple behaviour
sit/touch

Offer a medium Chew

Train a new trick

Offer a hard Chew

Calm puppy

Manage their world to set them up to succeed

One of the easiest ways to prevent something unwanted happening is to create situations and scenarios where it is unlikely to be able to happen in the first place - we've all heard that prevention is better than cure! Here's how we can create success for our puppies.

- Provide plenty of rest
- Regular meals
- Adequate exercise (physical and mental)
- Free access to chews
- Set up a play pen or puppy proof area
- Calm children with supervised interaction
- Don't wear loose fitting or floaty clothes
- Recognise when puppy doesn't want to interact and would prefer to be alone

It's your job to help your puppy be the best they can be. You can aim to control and manage puppy's world, what they're allowed access to and when they're allowed access to it, so that they are prevented from practising unwanted behaviour and therefore you are setting them up to succeed.

During this section of the book we will explore all the points above in more detail so that you have some pointers to create good scenarios.

PROVIDE PLENTY OF REST

Something that is so important but isn't always easy is to ensure we provide opportunities and encourage plenty of rest for your growing puppy. Puppies need, on average, anywhere between 15 -18 hours of sleep each day. Possibly even 20 hours! If you notice your puppy is tired and not getting enough sleep, they will be exactly like a human would be – more grumpy and tired, which leads to more bitey!

Making sure your puppy has enough sleep or enough rest time throughout the day, every day, will help to reduce puppy biting. Encourage children (and adults!) to 'let sleeping dogs lie' and not disturb them when they are resting.

We often think that more exercise will make them tired and sleep for longer but often it just creates an over-tired (and more bitey) puppy - the more sleep and rest the better!

REGULAR MEALS

A puppy's tummy is tiny and they burn a lot of energy so you need to make sure that they are having regular meals and never running on empty - they get HANGRY just like we do!

Try to avoid your puppy getting hungry which again could result in being more tired and lead to nipping and mouthing.

It is recommended to feed your puppy 3 – 4 times a day up to the age of 6 months.

ADEQUATE EXERCISE
(PHYSICAL AND MENTAL)

Puppies should not over-exercise or engage in too many high impact activities whilst growing, so it may be that you feel you cannot physically 'wear them out'. Puppies are great at 'zooming' after games and walks, and trick us into thinking they are not yet tired, so we give them more exercise and stimulation – when often this is an 'over-aroused' response from a puppy who does not yet have the skills to know when to settle and switch off. It is our job to help them by encouraging calm desired behaviours.

You need to help them have outlets for that desire to be a puppy. Gentle exercise is recommended whilst they are still growing and developing - this will exclude long walks or high-impact, high-energy activities. You can actively encourage shorter walks, sniffy walks, mooching, calm activities (sniffing games) and interactions so that the potential excess energy is channelled into a calm mindset rather than ramped up into excitement.

Providing adequate mental exercise and stimulation opportunities throughout the day as part of your routine means we are always promoting a calmer energy, rather than undertaking lots of high-arousal activities and then trying to constantly calm down an excitable (and probably bitey) puppy.

Mental stimulation is worth a lot more than physical and it provides a feeling of satisfaction - rather than a worn-out puppy, you end up with a content puppy. Aiming to increase, or introduce mental stimulation for your dog will help reduce puppy biting. Some of the main reasons for nipping are boredom, having too much energy or undertaking too many overexciting activities - so finding fun ways to exercise their brain such as sniffing or searching for their food will help to stimulate them and reduce the need to puppy bite.

ACCESS TO CHEWS

Puppies need to use their strong jaws so we should make sure we give them plenty of access to chews. This may be by giving them a long-lasting chew in their pen/crate or giving free access with a 'chew box' in the house, which contains items that you're happy for puppy to help themselves to whenever they feel like they need to chew.

Often, we hand our dog a chew at a specific time but if they don't want to chew at that moment it's not helping them to learn what to do when they DO want to chew on something. Therefore, having a box of chews always available will teach puppy that they can go and take out a chew whenever they want to, and they will subsequently learn to settle themselves down to enjoy it.

Supervision when chewing is important, especially for young puppies so make sure someone is always there keeping an eye on them.

** A free access chew box may be not suitable in certain circumstances such as multi dog households, if there are resource guarding issues or if young children are present.

SET UP A PUPPY PROOFED CHILL ZONE

One of the more essential items when you have a puppy is play pen or a puppy proof area. Essentially, this is a safe place where you can leave puppy that encourages a calm space to relax. This is separate to their crate if you are crate-training your puppy. This area is theirs and has everything they may need but is away from the stimulation of people giving puppy a chance to rest as well.

Place the pen or use an area which is in a busy part of the house such as the living room, so that they are still part of the family and not shut away, they can still feel involved but also learn that calm energy is required in the living space.

Essentially, our goal is to be able to leave puppy in their playpen or puppy proof area, ensuring they are safe and have enough activities while learning to co-habit without interacting. It is useful not just for puppy biting but also for alone training, whilst you are eating, when you have guests, when you are unable to actively supervise and many more situations.

If you know your puppy is about to become excitable where nipping is more likely, you can encourage them into their area and provide mind games and chews, so that they are already working on calmness.

If they are already excitable and begin to mouth, a playpen creates a barrier between you and them, making it easier for you to move away and prevents the opportunity to grab onto trouser legs or chase children. It teaches them that the only reinforcement/satisfaction when you are in a bitey mood comes from chews not people.

CALM CHILDREN WITH SUPERVISED INTERACTION

If you have children, you will know that they are the best toy EVER from puppy's perspective. Puppies love it because they squeal and run with them like a big, fun chew toy! Children particularly younger children, don't necessarily understand that their actions make puppy's excitement worse and encourages unwanted behaviours.

As the main caregivers, you need to ensure ALL interactions between puppy and children are actively supervised to make sure it is a positive experience, and to help puppy to learn how to behave around children. If you aren't able to give 100% attention to the situation place your puppy in their pen.

One of the most useful tools in creating a safe space for puppies and children to interact is having a puppy playpen. This can be used in multiple ways to control and manage situations, including:

- Putting the pen around puppy while he is sleeping, so that children can not disturb him
- Putting the pen around the children while they are eating so that puppy can't beg or steal food which may not be suitable for them
- Encouraging children and puppy to spend time in the same room without interacting with each other

An important part of puppy training that is often overlooked, is teaching ALL family members, especially young children, how to appropriately interact with their new friend and how to respond to certain behaviours. Ensuring consistency from everyone is key to teaching puppy how to interact with their humans.

CLOTHING CHOICES

Many new puppy owners experience puppy yanking at their trouser leg whilst walking along. That's why managing what clothing you wear can be important.

Floaty clothing that wiggles and flows in the breeze can make puppy think it's an invitation for them to play. Likewise, fluffy slippers can easily be mistaken for a soft toy, look inviting and good to chew, and at this age puppies cannot yet differentiate between a fluffy toy and a fluffy slipper. For the first few months when you bring puppy home, don't wear anything that your puppy could see as an invitation to play and get silly with, such as loose fitting or floaty clothes, dressing gowns with belts dangling and shoes with laces.

If we teach them that these things aren't interesting, they won't discover it is rewarding or practice an unwanted behaviour, and therefore are unlikely to do it in the future.

LET PUPPY LEAD YOU

It's important to recognise when your puppy doesn't want to interact with you and would prefer to be alone. If puppy is engaged in an activity or settled and we go over to try and interact with them, the only way they can tell you to leave them alone may be to give you a nip. So, it's important to recognise when puppy doesn't want to be played with or are happy occupying themselves.

Always aim to give your puppy a choice – invite them over to you before interacting, encourage them on to your lap rather than picking them up or forcing interaction. If you pick puppy up and they start nibbling and biting your hand, this is likely a sign they didn't want to be picked up in the first place. They have no other way to communicate this - nipping hands is the only thing that works and gives them back their own space so they soon learn to keep doing it. If we respect their choice and autonomy first they won't have to ask us to stop.

TOP TIP: If you are picking your puppy up to remove them from certain situations, focus heavily on a strong name association or recall to prevent the need to pick them up

LET SLEEPING DOGS LIE

Some of the more well-known sayings can be taken with a pinch of salt but others really are ones to listen to – if your puppy is already asleep, leave them unless you absolutely have to disturb them (and just because you want a cuddle or to play isn't a good enough reason!). No one likes to be woken up abruptly and that includes your puppy.

Be Prepared!

"Failing to prepare is preparing to fail"
Benjamin Franklin

Always have the tools you need available and easily accessible so that you can use them at the exact moment you need them, rather than having to go and find them.

- Have your puppy pen area set up at all times, ensure the items your puppy needs are in there waiting for them

- Keep a super yummy edible chew in your pocket

- Have food rewards/treats in your pocket, wear a treat pouch or have a jar full in every room (you could use their regular food if dry)

- Keep a fun tuggy toy in your pocket

Puppies and dogs live in the moment and for success we need to live in the moment too. It's important to make sure you have exactly what you need in exactly the right moment.

Aim to be proactive and prevent puppies from needing to mouth and/or bite in the first place!

How to prevent biting

Puppies mouth and nip for a reason. It is extremely rare for them to suddenly begin to do so without warning or an explanation, often we just don't see it or understand their reasons for doing so.

We recommend keeping a diary - that way if you aren't sure what the reason is, you can see if there is a pattern or correlation between events that is making your puppy have days/periods where they are more likely to nip or mouth, or become worse at certain times.

In this section we will explore the common reasons that puppies may become more bitey:

- Tiredness
- Over stimulation/ over excited
- Overwhelm
- Boredom
- Teasing
- Hunger
- Witching Hour

TIREDNESS

Tiredness is one of the most common reasons that puppies may mouth/nip. Think of an overtired toddler: they haven't learned yet that sleep is a good idea and they will try and fight it to the end. Puppies are the same.

Tiredness can play a massive part in puppy biting and so ensuring they have had enough sleep will help. Learning to recognise when they're getting tired means that you can encourage and promote sleep, give them a nice, yummy chew or encourage them into the playpen and give them some calm activities to help them chill out, thus avoiding the over-tired nipping phase.

TOP TIP: Don't be tricked into thinking a bitey puppy has not been exercised enough - usually it's the opposite!

OVER-STIMULATION / EXCITED

Another reason your puppy may bite is because they are overstimulated or over-excited. Maybe.......
- They've been playing for too long?
- They've had too many fun things to do?
- Walked for too long?
- Seen lots of new things?
- Someone just arrived at the house?

For a puppy all of these things are super exciting and stimulating, remember they are still learning and they don't know how to manage such big emotions. Nipping and biting can generally make them feel better. Identifying which situations or events are causing them to be overstimulated will help you recognise the triggers and learn to avoid or minimise those situations.

BOREDOM

Sometimes they could just be bored and have nothing else to do. We can help alleviate this by providing mental stimulation, exercise, games, interaction and/or training. Dogs are opportunists and, if not given opportunity to have a job or role will find their own employment – often this is by attempting to 'play' with people or trouser legs, but could also be by ripping up cushions or chewing on your trainers.

BEING TEASED

Puppy may start nipping and biting more if they are being or have been teased. This could be from little children offering toys and them moving them away or offering treats and taking them away for fear of being nipped. Let's face it; adults may do this too but being aware of it will help to prevent it. We don't want to teach them that 'when I tease you and don't give you what I'm offering' that you should nip me.

AVOID HUNGER

It's important to highlight - they may be hungry - it may just be before dinner time, or they've just had dinner which is super exciting, but food hasn't got to their tummy yet. Feeding regular small meals will prevent that tummy from ever getting empty and the resulting HANGER. Remember training treats, food games and chewing all keep that tummy full.

> **Top Tip**
> Encourage children and more wary adults to feed puppy a treat in an open hand (like you would if feeding sheep at the farm) to avoid puppy accidentally nipping fingers. If you are worried about nipped fingers you are likely to move your hands away quickly, which encourages puppies and dogs to snatch quickly and increases the risk of nipping - it's a vicious circle

OVER-WHELM

They may be overwhelmed. It's strange to think of a young puppy being overwhelmed, but remember the world is a big, new place with so many new and unusual things for them to encounter, both positive and negative. Your puppy may have only been sat at the café under the table BUT they will have seen so many people, animals, birds, objects, heard new sounds and slept with one eye open. This all adds to their 'emotional cup' and can be a factor towards inducing puppy biting.

It is worth noting that emotions and stress are cumulative and it can take a few days for your puppy to reduce their stress from a previous day. If your puppy had a busy day on Sunday but a relatively quiet day on Monday and is super bitey, it is not coming 'out of nowhere', it is a reaction and release of energy from the previous day's activities.

WITCHING HOUR

It may just be that it's Witching Hour, which many puppy owners may have experienced before. It tends to be early evening, either just before or just after dinner, where your puppy seems a little bit possessed – running round and doing zoomies until at the end of it they just flop. Whilst it is quite common – some puppies do it and some puppies don't – but those that do, tend to grow out of it eventually.

My personal view is that it's just the end of the day and they've had a busy, overstimulating, overwhelming day and they're just tired and need to get out that last bit of emotion/overwhelm before settling for the evening.

If witching hour is happening as regular as clockwork, think about how we can show them a better way to release all those pent-up emotions – food searching games, chewing etc.

If you are unsure what the reason is
KEEP A DIARY!

As mentioned these are common reasons, it is by no means exhaustive as all puppies are unique, however these will help you to narrow down the possibilities.

Reflecting on your last few days and thinking about these reasons will help you to see if any resonate with you.

If you aren't sure why your puppy is biting it's a good idea to keep a diary and make a note of
- what has happened in the day(or previous days)
- what times they ate
- walks and outings
- people arriving/leaving the home

Having a written schedule and noting when mouthing is worse will help you to reflect on the last day and see if there are any patterns emerging. For example that biting starts just as you come home, or just before mealtimes, or when guests arrive at your home.

Your diary, will help you identify any patterns and then you have the knowledge to predict behaviour and can work to prevent it.

By being proactive in your approach you can prevent puppies from needing to mouth/bite in the first place, thus eradicating the need to stop them!

Puppies mouth and bite for a reason. It is extremely rare for them to suddenly begin to do so without warning or an explanation, often we just don't see it or understand their reasons for doing so.

WHY IS MY PUPPY BITEY?

COULD THEY BE OVER TIRED? DO THEY NEED A REST?

YES → ENCOURAGE REST / SLEEP

NO ↓

HAVE THEY JUST BEEN FOR A WALK OR HAD A NEW EXPERIENCE

NO → HAVE YOU JUST FINISHED PLAYING WITH THEM

YES → PROVIDE SOME CALMING ACTIVITIES - SNIFFING OR FUN FQOD GAMES

NO → IS IT WITCHING HOUR?

YES → PROVIDE SOME CALMING ACTIVITIES - SNIFFING OR FUN FQOD GAMES

NO → ARE THEY BORED?

YES → PROVIDE SOME MENTAL STIMULATION

NO → GIVE THEM SOMETHING TO CHEW ON

Puppy Diary

Time	Activity	Biting 1/10 1 = none 10 = lot

What to do when biting happens

You can do your best to prevent your puppy feeling the need to mouth and nibble and of course it is always going to be easier and more effective to manage their world and their emotions so they never get to that bitey stage. But we're only human and sometimes, especially in the early days when you are still getting to grips with life with a puppy, you are going to miss the warning signs.

This section will look at how to manage situations when your puppy becomes that little land shark!

Just before the biting starts

When you notice the warning signs that puppy is about to start getting mouthy or bitey, try to interrupt and redirect before it escalates. We can do this by redirecting your puppy's attention on to another task which will channel their focus. They should find these activities equally as rewarding which teaches them a new behaviour to seek out in future similar situations. Not only this but these activities are also calming and relaxing so will promote a more level state of mind.

You can help to relieve stress and promote a calmer state of mind by encouraging your puppy to undertake the following magic trio of activities:

Licking

Licking is a primitive action which can be linked to suckling so provides a relaxing sensation

You can try:
putting some food on a licki-mat
placing some wet food in a kong
smearing puree pumpkin or yoghurt on a licki-mat or bowl

Chewing

Chewing stimulates the jaw and helps to relieve frustration
It also releases relaxing chemicals to promote calmness

You can try:
to offer a yummy chew

Sniffing

Sniffing stimulates a dog's strongest sense. The process uses approximately 40% of a dog's brain and has a calming and relaxing effect

You can try:
Sprinkling some treats in a snuffle mat or onto the grass
Lay a trail of treats around the house
Placing treats in fun feeding games and puzzles

When soft biting is initiated

If you miss the initial signs and land shark mode is activated, our main task is to refocus your puppy's attention into a new activity before the biting escalates. It's important to make sure the distraction activity you offer is like for like so we can help reward or distract our puppy by offering something similar.

Excitable

If puppy comes running over all excited looking at your trouser leg that they want to tug and play with, pull out a tug toy and let them tug on that instead. Essentially, we are telling them that if they feel like tugging they can tug on this toy and not a trouser leg. Once the initial excited energy is channelled we can then transition them into a calmer activity such as sniffing.

Gentle mouthing

If you start stroking puppy and teeth come into contact with your hand or they start to try and mouth you a little bit – they may be showing you that they are in a chewy mood and need a chew. At that point, you can offer them a yummy chew and teach them that if you want to chew, you chew on this.

Boredom/looking for engagement

If you notice puppy is starting to get a little bit mischievous because they are craving interaction, they may become a little bit bitey or nibbly, but they are still able to think and are not past the point of no return - ask them to do something.

Keep it super easy – don't ask them to do a fancy trick you only started learning yesterday as that is likely to be frustrating rather than easy. Instead, try reinforcing their name or ask for a paw. We would not recommend always using 'sit' because it can be overused – instead, just say their name (name association) and reward them, repeat and get their focus back on something else.

Not only are we channelling their energy into something other than puppy bitey, we are also showing our puppy that these activities are just as rewarding, if not more so, than nipping and biting you.

Rather than stopping them from biting, we're showing them an alternative. This teaches them that when you feel like this you should do this, rather than waiting for them to start nipping and biting and then taking them away from it. We want them to learn that nipping and biting is not rewarding but more appropriate activities are. Over time and as they develop they will learn how to self-regulate their emotions and make good choices in the future.

In summary:
· TUG – if puppy is aiming for trouser legs, pull out their favourite tuggy toy
· CHEW – if they appear in a chewing mood, as they start to think about mouthing/biting, offer a yummy chew
· TREAT – Ask for something they can do and reward with a treat or two.

Rather than stopping them from mouthing/biting, we are showing them what they should do when they feel this way and teaching them alternative methods to satisfy their needs. Essentially, we need to redirect them appropriately first and then transition them into a more suitable activity to promote calmness.

When you completely missed the warnings

Despite your best efforts, at some point you will miss the initial warning signs and puppy begins to mouth or bite. How we react to this can make all the difference in our success.

What NOT to do:

- Yelp, squeal, run away – this becomes a game and is rewarding
- Tap them on the nose/get cross – puppies won't understand this and it can encourage more biting
- Tell them off – puppies may well stop but only because they are scared or feel threatened (again this can encourage more biting in response). This is detrimental and could result in your puppy losing trust in you - a good relationship with your dog is essential.
- Put puppy in their crate – the crate should be a safe place, not used as punishment

TOP TIP: you can place your puppy in their crate/pen when you notice the initial change in energy before biting happens to help them relax but not directly in response to biting

What you SHOULD do

- Stop interaction – take hands away, stop fussing, stand up, walk away, leave the room (stairgates/pens can help here)
- Scatter a handful of treats onto the floor – redirecting and encouraging them to calm/relax
- Use a houseline (thin, short and light weight lead) – to guide puppy to a better choice or lead them to another room
- Understand their body language cues – if you can understand your dog and what they're saying to you it will help to pre-empt situations

By repeating these actions often, your puppy will learn that when they are bitey the person will leave and this is a direct consequence of their action.

Training Games

As we have discovered, puppy's biting is usually emotional and development based and therefore there is no specific training activity or game that will directly prevent your puppy biting.

However there are a number of activities that will help to change their associations with hands and create more positive links to hands being more than just a chew toy.

Always undertake training activities when your puppy is calm, relaxed and happy NOT when they are in a bitey mood, overtired or over excited. It's important to always aim to set them up to succeed, so it is best to wait until they are in their right frame of mind to learn.

Puppies only have a very small attention span and get tired quite quickly, so keep training sessions short. About a minute is perfect to start with and then let them rest before trying again.

Practice as often as you can: life is busy so if twice a week is all you can manage that's fine. Even if you have loads of time, a maximum of once or twice a day is enough, we don't want to overdo it because remember sleep and rest are important too!

Name Game

The aim of this is to create a positive association with your puppy's name. Once learnt it will enable them to easily refocus their attention onto you when you say their name.

Step 1
Take 10 small treats.

Step 2
Say your puppy's name and offer them one food reward/treat 1-2 seconds after. Repeat with all 10 treats

They don't have to do anything; we're simply pairing their name with a positive linked to you.

Step 3
Repeat step 1 and 2 - however on every third treat, have a small pause after saying their name to see what they do – if they look up at you, we know they're starting to make an association – reward them. If they don't look up – still offer them the treat to continue to build the association and keep practicing.

Practice once or twice a day and always give a food reward to continue strengthening their name!

Avoid using their name harshly or to tell them off as this will undo the positive association you are forming

Nose target

The main aim of this is to create a positive connection with hands, however it can also be used to re-direct your puppy's nose into a new position and take their attention away from biting.
It is quite a simple behaviour so even when puppy is over tired it can easily be performed.

Step 1
Hold your hand out in a flat open palm (palm facing your dog) and place a treat between your thumb and forefinger.

Step 2
Move your hand to around 6 inches in front of your dog's nose. As they move in towards the treat (keep your hand still) and you feel their wet nose against your hand, release the treat.

Repeat 5 times.

Step 3
Hold your flat palm out but without a treat between your fingers, wait for your puppy to move their nose towards your hand. As they make contact, praise and produce a treat from behind your back.

If Step 3 is too hard, move back to Step 2 and gradually shift from having a treat or no treat in your palm - always reward them.

The hand becomes a cue for 'place your nose upon my hand'

Practice once a day for around a minute

Handling

The aim of handling is to firstly create a positive association with hands providing affection and stroking rather then being something to bite on. Secondly they help your puppy get used to and comfortable being touched by people, which will prepare them for grooming, body inspections and future care.

Step 1
Wait for a time when your puppy is calm and relaxed, chilling out but not asleep. Find a comfy spot on the floor/sofa together

Step 2
Prepare yourself with a handful of treats

Step 3
Choose a part of the body, e.g the back (start easy) and gently stroke from top to bottom - offer a small food reward after the stroke.
Repeat 2 or 3 times

Step 4
Repeat including head, ears, legs, tail, bottom, eyes, nose, gums

To begin with these are just a gentle stroke in non-intrusive areas. Stroke = reward.
This should only take a few minutes maximum, a few times per week and always in a calm, relaxed and positive way. Over time you can begin to simulate 'inspections' and grooming of areas.

Rewards create happy positive emotions which will be paired with the touch and therefore ensure your puppy has a good association with hands approaching them

TOP TIP: Understanding your dog's body language is key!

Body Language

It's important to understand how your puppy communicates and in turn you learn how to respect their communication and respond accordingly.

This is important not just in handling but in ALL aspects of life with your puppy. Understanding how your dog communicates is vital to your future successes and relationship.

If your puppy shows any signs of being uncomfortable, dislikes your touch, begins mouthing or appears to be stressed – stop!

When handling, reduce your length and pressure of strokes to ensure they are comfortable

Signs of being uncomfortable can include
- showing the whites of the eyes
- licking lips
- lip twitching
- yawns

I would strongly recommend learning as much as possible about communication to ensure you are always able to understand how your dog is feeling in any given situation.

You can learn more about Canine Body Language via attending courses or reading books on the topic - see 'Useful Information' section for more information.

Play

Learning to play tug appropriately with your puppy will help them to manage their arousal and learn some toy manners.

It may seem obvious how to play with a puppy, grab a toy, tug and there you go – but a lot of learning happens through play so it's best to make sure you're doing it effectively and reinforcing good skills as early as possible.

Step 1
Find a toy that is long enough that both you and your puppy can hold one end each, and is something soft, like a classic tuggy and most importantly something your puppy seems to like!

Step 2
Wiggle the toy, keeping it low to the ground, to get your puppy interested in it and allow them chase it around a little

Step 3
When they grab it, gently tug from side to side, match your tug pressure to the enthusiasm of your dog – get invested and have a little 'grrrr' as you do!

Step 4
After a few seconds of tug - stop, hold the toy still and wait for puppy to lose interest and either let go of the toy or loosen their grip – they might need a little encouragement so sprinkle 2 or 3 treats into the floor. This is an exchange of toy for treats.

Step 5
Once you have the toy back wiggle the toy again to repeat the game. Only repeat a couple of times to ensure they don't become over-excited. End with a calming scatter feed

Summary

Prevention and understanding your puppy's needs and emotional state are crucial for reducing puppy biting. We are unlikely to eradicate it completely but we can channel their desires into more appropriate activities.

The tips and knowledge shared in this guide, are exactly that, a guide. Please remember that every puppy is individual so what works for one may not work for another and some methods may be preferred by either you or your puppy. If in doubt, do contact a reputable trainer to support you.

Puppy biting can be one of the hardest challenges to overcome but with regular practice and a proactive approach it will get better!

Remember, that all training will take time, patience and lots of consistency in your approach, so do keep persevering. Most puppies, with the right support and guidance, will grow out of mouthing/biting by around 6 months old.

And finally, enjoy your puppy!

Sharing your life with a dog (or three) is a wonderful opportunity to experience unconditional love, develop skills and learn more about yourself than you'd imagined.

You will learn together every day throughout your lives, not just in your initial puppy stages. Your dog is always developing and learning and that's why training is a journey you experience together.

That's why I believe

Training is for life, not just for puppies!

Discover more

If you have enjoyed this book and want to discover more about Debbie and training you can do so in the following ways:

Work with Debbie and her training team online or in-person
potterpaws.co.uk

Book a Training Chat with Debbie
debbiepotter.co.uk

Listen to Debbie's weekly podcast The Dynamic Dog Owner, available on all platforms including You Tube

thedynamicdogowner.co.uk

Glossary

Appropriate behaviours/play/activities	Actions that are appropriate to the situation
Arousal	When emotions or feelings become heightened and intense
Behaviour: **- Desired Behaviour** **- Undesired Behaviour**	A behaviour is an action that takes place. Desired/wanted is behaviour we like or want. Undesired/Unwanted is an action that we would prefer didn't happen
Body Inspections	Checking your dog's body for health purposes
Body Language	How dogs communicate through small movements of variou body parts
Canine Companion	A person who shares life with a dog
Chew Box	A box of chews available for dogs to choose for themselves
Cue	A word or visual sign that instructs a behaviour
Emotional cup	The volume of emotions a dog (or human) can hold before overreacting
Feeding Games/puzzles	Interactive games and activities centred around a dog's foo allowance and creatively obtaining it
Hangry	When being hungry makes you more irritable
High energy activity	An activity that generates lots of excitement or over-arousa like running, playing, chasing
Houseline	A thin lead that is left to trail whilst your dog is in the house
Kibble	Dog food consisting of dry biscuits
Kong	A hollow rubber 'toy' that can be stuffed with dry or wet food
Landshark	A puppy that bites like a shark but stays on land
Licki-mat	A silicone mat with an indented pattern which you can smea soft food onto for your puppy to lick off

Mental Stimulation	Activities that encourage your puppy to use their brain
Mooching	A slow relaxing walk where your puppy can sniff as much as they like and follow their nose
Mouthing	When your puppy gently holds and moves items around in their mouth/with their teeth - this can include hands - it does not hurt
Over-stimulation	When your puppy receives too much sensory input
Overwhelm	When emotions are too big to manage
Play Pen	A series of metal grill panels that are connected and can be placed into a variety of shapes to create a fenced area to keep your puppy in
Proofed area	A room or area within a room that is contained and safe from any dangers
Rawhide	A 'chew' item sold in pet shops that is the bi-product of the leader industry and is indigestible - it is not recommended for dogs
Food reward	Something edible we give to our dogs which provides a positive consequence to actions
Scatter Feed	Sprinkling treats onto the ground to encourage your dog to sniff them out
Sniffy Games	Games which encourage your dog to use their nose
Sniffy Walk	A walk where the primary focus is to allow your dog to sniff and choose the direction
Snuffle Mat	A mat with long strands of fleece which can have treats sprinkled on/in it for your dog to sniff out
Treat pouch	A pouch on a strap similar to a bum bag where you can store treats to enable you to reward your puppy easily
Trick	A behaviour that appears to be 'fancy' e.g. a spin
Tuggy Toy	A toy that is long enough for both human and puppy to hold on to at the same time to allow tugging
Witching Hour	A period of time in the day, usually early evening, when your puppy seems particularly mischievous
Zoomies	When puppies run around like crazy, usually in periods of over excitement or when overtired as a release of energy

Useful Information

Where to find a trainer

IMDT
https://www.imdt.uk.com/find-a-qualified-imdt-trainer

APDT
https://apdt.co.uk/find-a-trainer/

The Dog Training College
https://www.findadogtrainer.com/

More Reading

Doggie Language Book by Lili Chin
https://www.doggielanguagebook.com/

Resources

Where to buy chews
JR Pet Products - www.jrpetproducts.com
Finer by Nature - www.finerbynature.co.uk

Sources

https://en.wikipedia.org/wiki/Puppy_teething

Printed in Great Britain
by Amazon

47218425R00037